AUTHENTIC AMERICAN INDIAN BEADWORK
AND HOW TO DO IT

With 50 Charts for Bead Weaving and
21 Full-Size Patterns for Appliqué

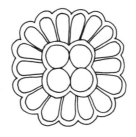

PAMELA STANLEY-MILLNER

Dover Publications, Inc.
New York

This book is dedicated with love
to my husband James
and my sons Clinton John
and Matthew Aaron.

Introduction

American Indian beadwork is on display in many museums around the country. Its splendid colors and vibrant patterns enlivening belts, dresses, headbands and other leather artifacts are a testament to the skill of many hands and the eye for beauty of many tribes. In the pages that follow, you will find complete instructions for two types of traditional American Indian bead application—bead weaving and appliqué beading—plus 71 authentic American Indian beadwork designs, 50 charted on graph paper for bead weaving and 21 drawn as full-size patterns for appliqué. You will find it possible to achieve the very striking effects you have admired and will be surprised to discover how simple the techniques are.

Beadcraft has such a long history in American Indian culture that the origin of many designs is obscure. Some bead designs are representational. For example, a cross symbolizes the four winds; a zigzag line, lightning. Characteristic designs differentiate the beadwork of one tribe from that of another. Some favor geometrics; others, florals; still others, animal depictions. Tribal origin is specified for each beadwork design included in this book. You will be able to see for yourself which tribes favor which motifs.

BEADS. In Columbus's day, coastal American Indians used shells, both in their natural state and shaped and polished into wampum, as the beads for their fancy work. Not long, however, after the arrival of the European settlers, French traders bartering with the Indians for furs introduced glass beads from Italy. These first glass beads, called pony beads, were eagerly adopted and soon incorporated in Indian beadwork and eventually replaced shell beads.

Pony beads were larger—five times larger—than the beads commonly in use today. The Indians fashioned them, despite their size, into elaborate necklaces and beaded patterns on fringed shirts and dresses. Pony beads have not disappeared, but the small glass seed bead—an import from Czechoslovakia—became popular around 1850 and remains the favorite to this day.

Both opaque and transparent seed beads are readily available in many different colors. They also come in various circumferences ranging from the largest, size 10 (10°), to the smallest, size 14 (14°). Size 12 beads are the most versatile: they can be used for both bead weaving and appliqué beading, the two techniques covered in this book. Almost all projects shown in color on the covers are worked with size 12 beads.

THREAD. The original thread for beadwork came from sinew, the tough, fibrous, connective tissue of animals. The American Indian split the sinew from deer and buffalo into strands fine enough for stringing beads; the prepared sinew is still available—

but something of a novelty—even today. When cotton threads became commercially available in the 1800s, they easily gained acceptance in beadwork. More recently they have been joined by nylon.

Cotton crochet thread No. 30 is recommended for warping the loom in bead weaving; it is readily available in needlework shops and at notion counters. Nylon thread Size 0, combining the virtues of strength and fineness, is ideal for the threaded needlework in both bead weaving and bead appliqué; but it is a craft specialty item that it may be necessary to order from suppliers such as the trading posts listed at the end of this introduction.

It is recommended, in both bead weaving and bead appliqué, to thread the needle in two-foot lengths at a time. In bead weaving this two-foot length is single strand; in bead appliqué, both two-foot lengths are double strand.

WAX. Whether using cotton or nylon thread in the needle, wax it to prevent tangles or breakage. A fine residual wax coat is all that's necessary to hold the thread fibers in place. Beeswax sold in cakes at sewing notion counters is excellent. Wax the full length of thread you'll be working with, first on one side and then on the other.

The *warp* threads in bead weaving do not need waxing: they are a three-stranded thread and therefore very unlikely to break, and they are held taut during the beading and cannot tangle.

NEEDLES. A needle specially designed for the purpose—a beading needle—is used in both bead weaving and bead appliqué to pick up the beads in pattern order. Longer and thinner than the average sewing needle, the beading needle will minimize broken beads and frayed threads. Averaging two inches in length, beading needles are available in Nos. 10 through 16—the higher the number, the thinner the needle. *No. 16* is recommended and is available from craft suppliers.

The *second* needle in appliqué beading must easily penetrate the material on which the design will be appliquéd (for example, garment leather or velvet). A No. 9 sharp, commonly available for hand sewing, is recommended.

MAIL ORDER SUPPLIERS. If the materials you need for beadwork are not available from local suppliers, the following trading posts will be able to help you by mail:

Western Trading Post
P.O. Box 9070
Denver, CO 80209-0070

Winona Trading Post
P.O. Box 309
Athens, TX 75751

Published in Canada by General Publishing Company, Ltd., 30 Lesmill Road, Don Mills, Toronto, Ontario.
Published in the United Kingdom by Constable and Company, Ltd.

Authentic American Indian Beadwork and How to Do It: With 50 Charts for Bead Weaving and 21 Full-Size Patterns for Appliqué is a new work, first published by Dover Publications, Inc., in 1984.

Manufactured in the United States of America
Dover Publications, Inc., 31 East 2nd Street, Mineola, N.Y. 11501

Library of Congress Cataloging in Publication Data

Stanley-Millner, Pamela.
     Authentic American Indian beadwork and how to do it.

     1. Beadwork 2. Indians of North America—Embroidery. 3. Indians of North America—Costume and adornment.
I. Title.
TT860.S73   1984   746.5   84-6035
ISBN 0-486-24739-2

Bead Weaving

Loom Construction.   The most important tool for bead weaving is a loom. Generally speaking, you can build a loom longer and wider than any you can buy. Greater loom length and width translates into larger bead weavings. Besides, constructing a loom is *easy*. The necessary wood, along with nails and screws, is readily available from a hardware store or lumberyard; it may even turn up among odds and ends you have at home. You will need the following wood and hardware: one 36″ × 7″ × ¾″ board (base of the loom);* two 11″ × 7″ × ¾″ boards (sides of the loom); 8 wood screws, 1½″ long; 2 medium-sized nails, ¾″ long.

Fasten the sides to the base with the screws (see *Fig. 1*). Space the screws evenly, four at each end, and tighten them securely. This is

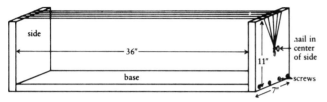

Figure 1: Bead Loom

crucial to the stability of the loom. Next, pound the nails into the side boards, one nail exactly in the center of each board on the outside. Leave the nails protruding ¼″ (see *Fig. 1*). The nails are essential for warping the loom. Last, the tops of the sides must be notched with very narrow incisions as illustrated in *Fig. 2*. Starting ⅜″ from one end and using a sharp knife, make the notches ¹⁄₁₆″ deep and ¹⁄₁₆″ apart. Use a ruler as a placement guide. Cut approximately 100 notches in the top of each side, leaving a ⅜″ margin at each end. These notches will space the warp threads and hold them in position.

The Warp Count.   Before you warp the loom, refer to the charted design from which you are planning to work. Each vertical line equals one warp thread. Check for the number of warp threads the design requires. For your convenience, this count is given under every bead-weaving chart in this volume. The warp count is always *one more* than the total number of beads across one horizontal row of the design.

To center the warp threads on the loom, divide the warp count in half. Then, along *both* sides of the loom, count that halved number of notches *from* the center toward either end; be sure to count in the same direction on both sides. Mark these parallel notches temporarily with a small piece of tape.

Warping the Loom.   To begin warping the loom, tie the end of the cotton crochet thread No. 30 to the nail on one side of the loom (see *Fig. 2*). Next, bring the thread up this same side and into the notch

Figure 2: Detail of Notches along Top of Side

you have marked. Holding the thread in the notch with a finger, extend the thread the length of the loom to the parallel notch you have marked on the other side. Pull the warp thread taut and secure it in position by wrapping it around the nail in this side (see *Fig. 1*). Continue in this manner, warping first in one direction and then in the other, always through the next set of parallel notches, wrapping around one nail and the other in turn, until you have the total number of warp threads necessary for the design. Again, as at the beginning, tie off the thread on a nail and cut.

*A common bead weaving is the belt. If you plan to fit waist sizes larger than 36 inches, make your loom with a longer base; or else plan to adjust the fit by extending the leather backing of the bead weaving.

The Charts.   In all 50 charts for bead weaving, each square on the chart equals one bead. As you weave, read the charts in horizontal rows from top to bottom, returning to the top of the chart for the repeat unless otherwise indicated. Read each row from left to right.

Each chart is accompanied by a key to the bead color represented by each symbol. The unmarked squares—the background—are beaded in white unless another color is specified.

Technique.   Thread the No. 16 beading needle with a two-foot single strand of Size 0 nylon thread (Remember to wax it). The warped loom is held across the lap, extending to the left and right, or may be supported on a table. A couple of inches from the left notches, tie the loose end of the nylon thread to the warp thread closest to you. Then, reading from left to right across the top row of the design chart, pick up, in order, with the point of the threaded needle, the number and color of beads needed to complete the first row of the design. Slide the beads down the nylon thread to the knot.

Next, pass the needle and thread carrying the strung beads *under* the warp threads from left to right (away from you) and hold the needle in back (on the right) so that the thread with the beads is fairly taut underneath the warp. With the index finger of your free hand, push up each bead in turn, from left to right (front to back), between a pair of warp threads. Eventually your index finger will be holding the entire row of beads in place.

The return of the threaded needle through the beads *above* the warp threads will secure the row. Work from right to left (back to front) in four- or five-bead sections until the entire row of beads is threaded above the warp threads as well as below (see *Fig. 3*). Then return to the chart for the second row, third and so on. Each row is worked the same way.

Figure 3: Bead Weaving

The thread in your needle will not last forever. If you don't have enough to pass *both* under *and* over the warp to secure an entire row of beads, go back one row and run the needle and thread *from* the outside edge through a half dozen or so beads. No knot is necessary; the tucked thread will hold. Cut off any loose end remaining. Then rethread the needle, wax the thread, but don't tie it to the warp. Instead, in the last row worked, run the needle and thread through a half dozen or so beads *to* the outside edge, securing the end in this way without a knot. Proceed to reading the next row of the chart and picking up the necessary beads in order.

Fit and Sizing.   The many belts shown on both the inside front and the back covers fulfill two essentials of strong impact: the design repetitions are not only complete but also symmetrically spaced along the total length. The ends join visually as well as functionally, as is necessary in a belt. When both fit and look are critical, plan ahead by checking the gauge—the number of beads to the horizontal inch and the number of rows to the vertical inch—and using it to your advantage.

Let's assume you wish to make a belt to fit a 25½″ waist and are not concerned about width. On the design chart you plan to use, the count of horizontal rows from the beginning to the end of one complete design is 25. By weaving a small sample with the beads you plan to use, you discover that there are 5 rows of beads to the inch. Dividing 25 by 5 yields the design length: 5″. Allowing ½″ of waist size for securing the belt ends together, your bead weaving 25″ long could conceivably consist of 5 design repetitions; but there would then be no space whatsoever in between. Four repetitions, however, would leave background space, 5″ altogether that would distribute evenly in 1″ units, 5 rows of background beads each. The choice is yours *before* the commitment of time and effort.

In many design charts, background can be added and subtracted as fit requires. In the few designs that run continuously, if you cannot adjust size by adding or subtracting a design repetition, you may need to switch to another size bead. Of course, you can always *add* length by means of the leather or other material used in the finishing of your bead weaving.

Binding Off and Finishing. 1″ masking tape is very handy for binding off a bead-weaving project at each end. While the completed piece is still on the taut warp threads of the loom, run the tape above and below the warp threads next to the first and last rows of beads. Press the tape-warp-tape sandwiches together; the warp threads, permanently secured against unraveling, can then be cut, leaving the masking tape seals at either end of your bead weaving. Fold the masking tape to the back of the design and stitch it down.

After masking tape is used to bind off, whip-stitch the bead weaving by hand to a strip of garment leather or other material longer than the beaded piece. The extending ends of backing become the ties for a belt or the mounting of a wall hanging. This style of finishing is very common, and a number of examples appear on the covers.

Binding off can also be accomplished, in part or altogether, by tapering the ends of a bead weaving through decreases. Examples will be found on the covers. Beginning a project with increases is difficult and fortunately unnecessary: leave enough room on the warp threads at the beginning of the project to go back and decrease *after* having completed the rest of the piece. Leave space for as many rows as the number of beads to be decreased.

Let's assume you are working background rows and wish to decrease from 12 beads to 6. Pick up 10 beads for the next row, and double up warp threads between the first and the last two beads. Work another row 10 beads wide. Continue in this manner, decreasing 2 beads per row every other row—two rows of 8, two rows of 6—until the tapering is complete.

If the bead weaving will be backed, proceed with binding off and finishing as above, with the possible addition of an overhand knot where the ties begin. If the bead weaving will not be backed, cut the warp threads, leaving ends long enough to tie in an overhand knot and/or tuck back into previous rows of beads.

Appliqué Beading

Once you choose a design for bead appliqué, place tracing paper over the full-size pattern in the book, secure it with paper clips and copy in pen or pencil. Don't copy the color key numbers in the pattern; it's easier to refer to them in the book as you work.

It's also necessary to choose the material on which to bead appliqué. Suede, garment leather and velvet are all suitable for bead appliqué; the project—purse, vest, wall hanging—will determine what's best. Keep in mind whether the bead colors in the pattern will stand out on the color background you choose. If the background material must be a given color, you may wish to adjust bead colors for a stronger effect.

Once you have a pattern tracing and material to work on, you're ready to transfer the pattern from the tracing to the material. Work on a piece of material *larger* than the finished dimensions of the project; cut to size *after* the appliqué beading. Place the material right side up on a flat surface. Next, place a sheet of carbon paper—larger than the pattern—on the material, carbon side down, followed by the pattern tracing, tracing side up. Holding all three layers securely in position, firmly retrace the entire pattern with pen or pencil; the pressure should transfer a carbon outline of the pattern to the material for bead appliqué. No special carbon paper is required; you may use dressmaker's carbon if you prefer, especially if you need a *light* outline on a *dark* material.

Once the design is transferred and the material is ready for appliqué, stretch it taut in an embroidery hoop or stapled to a frame. Use the color key accompanying the pattern in the book as a guide to the bead colors you will need. Size 0 nylon thread, a No. 16 beading needle, a No. 9 sharp needle, scissors and beeswax—once gathered together, you're ready to begin.

In beading all design elements, outline first, then fill in the interiors. Whether to outline with one, two or three rows of beads is determined by overall design proportions. Bead the interiors along lines that enhance the look of a given motif. Study the finished bead appliqué projects on the front and the inside back covers for examples of interiors beaded to advantageous effect. You will also notice variations in outlining.

Thread each needle with a double strand of nylon thread two feet long, ends knotted together. Remember to wax it. Begin with the beading needle. Draw it from the back to the front of the stretched

material, and pull until the knot is tight against the back. Do this at a point in the pattern where it is logical to begin laying down beads to outline a design element (for example, a leaf, a petal, a bud). Then string enough beads on the thread to cover the outline of this design element, but not so many that there won't be a loose end of thread with which to tie off.

Now take up the other needle, the No. 9 sharp. If you are right-handed, work this needle with your right hand; if left-handed, favor this needle with your left. Bring the sharp up from the back of the material in the same manner as the beading needle, but positioned to tack the bead-carrying thread to the design outline between the first and second beads. Proceed accordingly: go back through the material, completing the tacking of the first thread with the second thread between the first and second beads (see *Fig 4*). The appliqué of the first bead is complete.

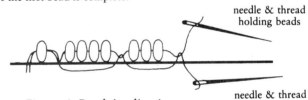

needle & thread holding beads

needle & thread securing beads

Figure 4: Bead Appliqué

The remaining beads are secured in the same fashion but in intervals of three or four beads between tacks. Just be sure to tack frequently enough that the beads hold the outline of the design. Follow this procedure throughout the appliqué project, even for filling in the interiors of the design.

When either thread is running out, pull it through to the wrong side of the material and knot, either by chain stitching or by tying to other threads on the wrong side. *Don't knot to the material:* this would show on the right side. Rethread your needle, wax the thread and continue, checking the color key of the pattern for what beads to use next.

Once the bead appliqué is complete, release the material from the embroidery hoop or stretcher frame, cut to the necessary dimension for your project and hand or machine sew the finished piece.

The Designs

All designs rendered for bead weaving and appliqué beading were copied from American Indian artifacts found in museum collections in the United States. The following museums graciously consented to the inclusion of the designs on the following pages:

Field Museum of Natural History, Chicago, Illinois: 6 (Osage), 12 (Sauk & Fox), 14 (right), 16, 17, 19 (Chippewa, Iroquois), 22 (Arikara), 25 (Potawatomi), 26 (Osage), 31–33.
Milwaukee Public Museum, Wisconsin: 5, 6 (Woodland), 7, 14 (left), 24, 26 (Woodland), 27, 30, 38, 40, 48.
The Montclair Art Museum, New Jersey: 12 (Chippewa), 22 (Chippewa), 23 (Winnebago), 25 (Winnebago), 34–37.

Museum of the American Indian, Heye Foundation, New York, New York: 8, 9, 13, 15 (Winnebago), 21, 28, 39, 41–46.
New Jersey State Museum, Trenton: 11, 15 (Delaware), 20.
Department of Anthropology, Smithsonian Institution, Washington, D.C.: 10, 15 (Crow), 18, 19 (Sioux), 23 (Crow), 29, 47.

You are invited to see the original beadwork for yourself.

You will also find the designs adaptable to other crafts. The bead-weaving charts are ready for use in needlepoint, counted cross-stitch, latch-hooking, crochet and knitting; the full-size patterns for bead appliqué can also be used in fabric appliqué, embroidery of many kinds and painting on wood or fabric.

Charts for Bead Weaving

WOODLAND

60 warp threads

COLOR KEY   ⊠ brown   ⊡ pink

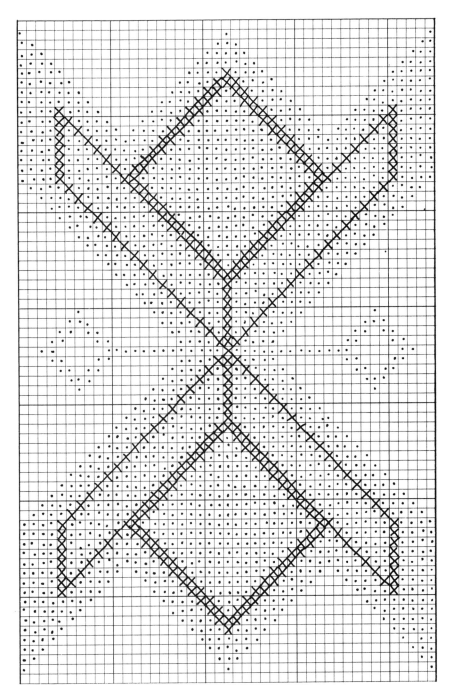

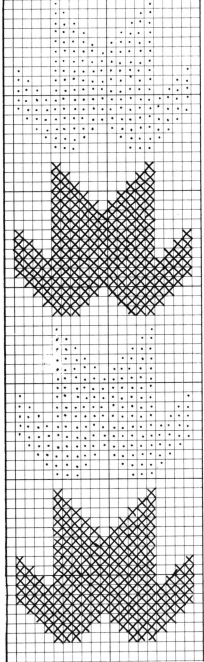

OSAGE

46 warp threads

COLOR KEY ⊠ yellow   · blue

WOODLAND

Shown in color on the back cover.

22 warp threads

COLOR KEY ⊠ blue   · turquoise
background—yellow

WOODLAND
Shown in color on the inside front and inside back covers.

66 warp threads

COLOR KEY   ☑ dark green   ☒ red
                ⊡ yellow   ⊙ blue

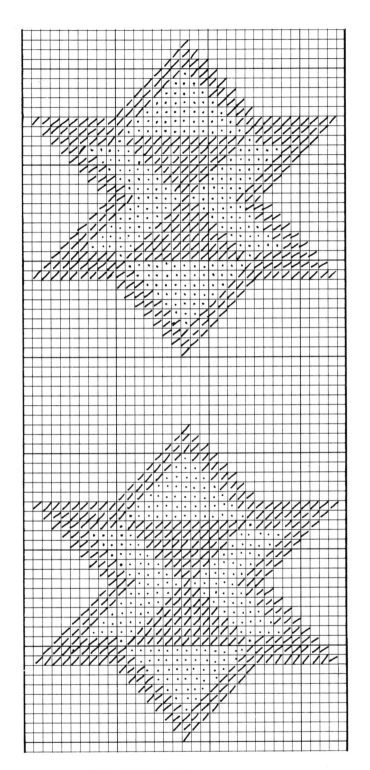

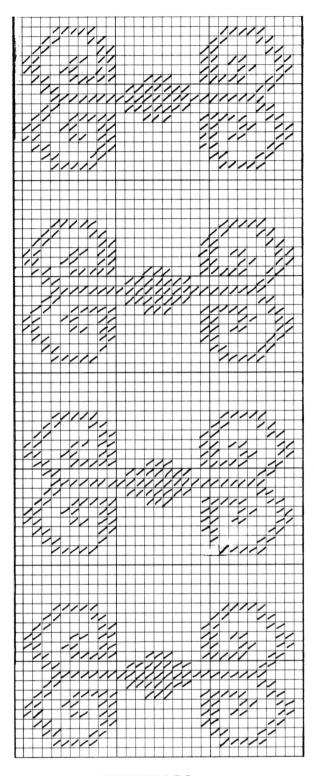

WINNEBAGO

36 warp threads

COLOR KEY ⊘ red ⊡ blue

WINNEBAGO

32 warp threads

COLOR KEY ⊘ red

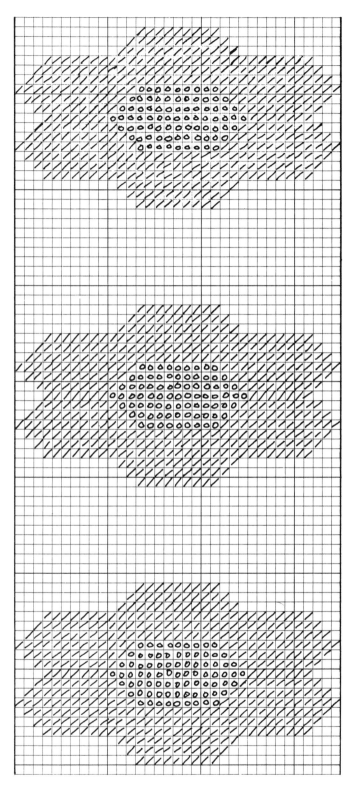

WINNEBAGO
Shown in color on the back cover.

36 warp threads
COLOR KEY ⊙ yellow ⊘ blue

KICKAPOO
Shown in color on the back cover.

19 warp threads
COLOR KEY ⊘ red ⊙ light blue
background—blue

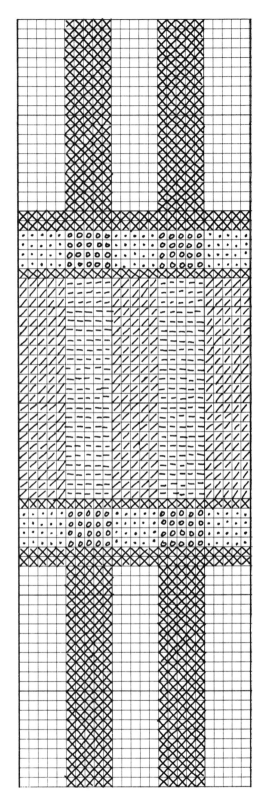

CROW

26 warp threads

COLOR KEY   ☒ black   ⊟ yellow
                ⊡ light blue   ☑ red
                ⊙ pink

CROW

Shown in color on the inside front cover.

36 warp threads

COLOR KEY   ⊡ red   ☑ yellow
                ⊙ pink
                background—light blue

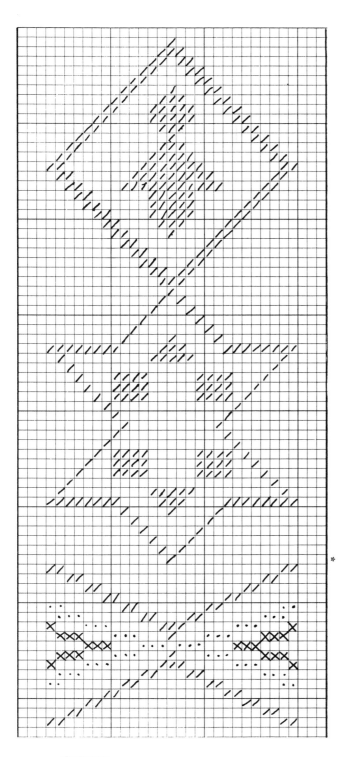

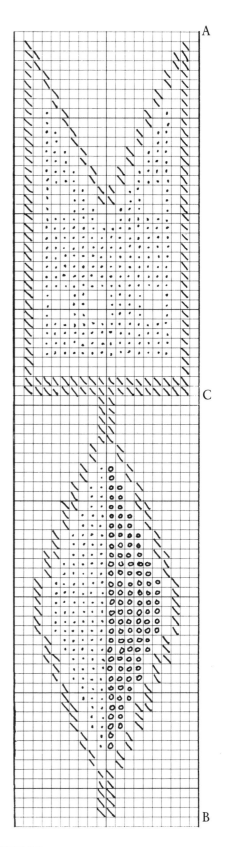

SIOUX

34 warp threads

COLOR KEY   · red   ◪ white

              ⊠ orange

              background—royal blue

*Begin repeat in reverse.

SIOUX

Shown in color on the back cover.

21 warp threads

COLOR KEY   ◩ red   · navy blue

              ⊙ green

Work A to B, then C to A for

complete motif.

11

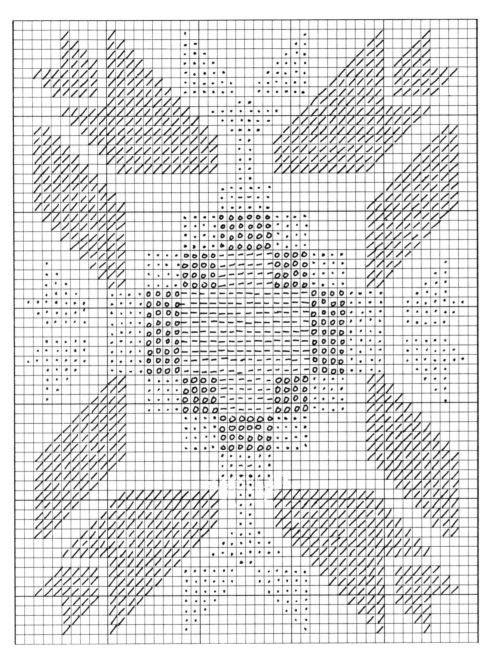

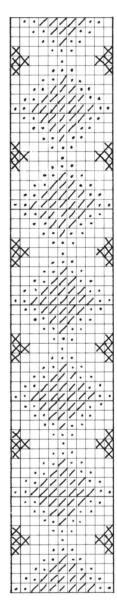

SAUK & FOX

51 warp threads

COLOR KEY   ⧄ red   ⊟ yellow

                ⊡ black   ⊙ orange

CHIPPEWA

12 warp threads

COLOR KEY   ☒ gold

                ⊡ dark green

                ⧄ light green

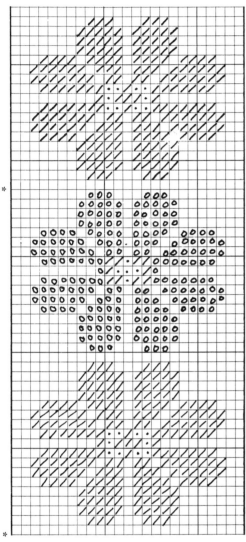

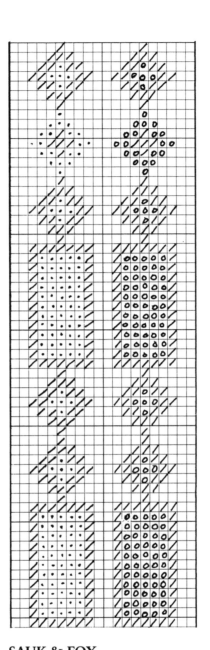

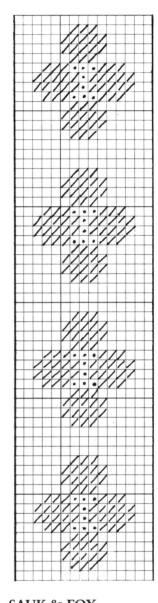

SAUK & FOX

Shown in color on the back cover.

26 warp threads

COLOR KEY   ⊡ pearl   ⊙ yellow

           ⊘ black

Repeat from * to * for pattern.

SAUK & FOX

21 warp threads

COLOR KEY   ⊘ black   ⊡ red

                ⊙ yellow

SAUK & FOX

16 warp threads

COLOR KEY   ⊘ light blue

            ⊡ red

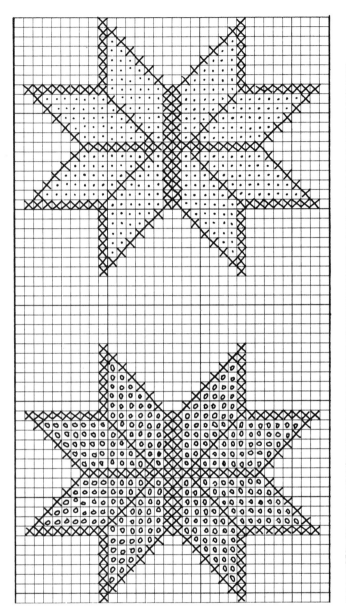

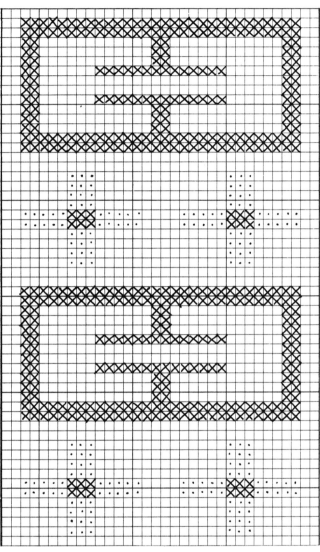

WOODLAND

35 warp threads

COLOR KEY ☒ brown ⊡ pink
⊙ green

WOODLAND

35 warp threads

COLOR KEY ☒ navy blue ⊡ red

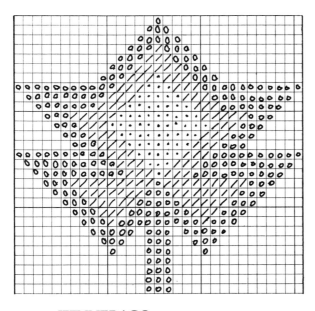

WINNEBAGO

32 warp threads

COLOR KEY   ⊙ blue   ⧄ green

          ⊡ red

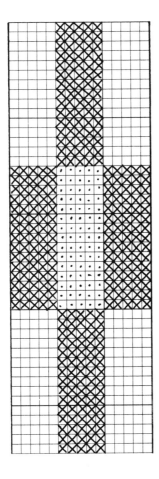

CROW

16 warp threads

COLOR KEY   ⊠ medium blue   ⊡ light blue

          background—pink

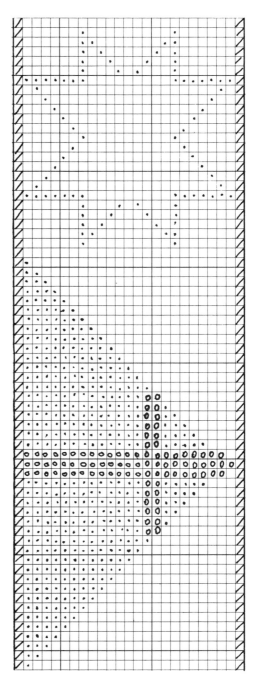

DELAWARE

Shown in color on the inside front cover.

26 warp threads

COLOR KEY   ⊙ yellow   ⧄ royal blue

          ⊡ white

          background—red

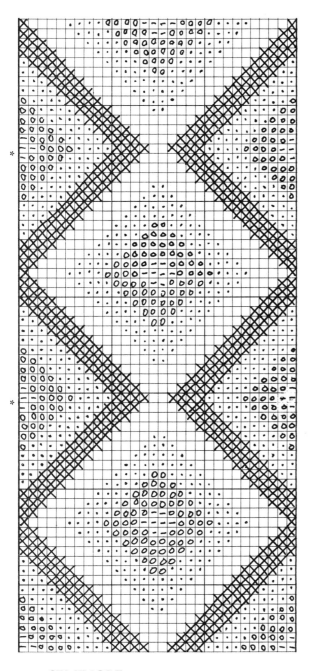

SEMINOLE

Shown in color on the front cover.

31 warp threads

COLOR KEY   ⊠ blue   ⊡ red

                 ⊡ orange   ⊟ yellow

Repeat from * to * for pattern.

SEMINOLE

Shown in color on the inside front cover.

31 warp threads

COLOR KEY   ⊠ brown   ⊡ blue

                 ◣ black   ⊟ orange

                 ⊡ green   ⫿ yellow

                 ◢ red

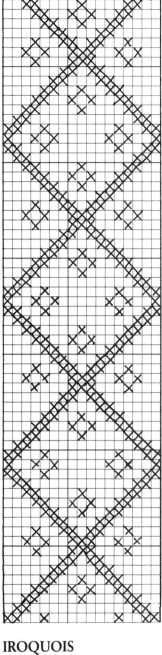

PAWNEE

51 warp threads

COLOR KEY ⊠ black ⊡ green
· orange ⧄ yellow

IROQUOIS

18 warp threads

COLOR KEY ⊠ black
background—
light blue

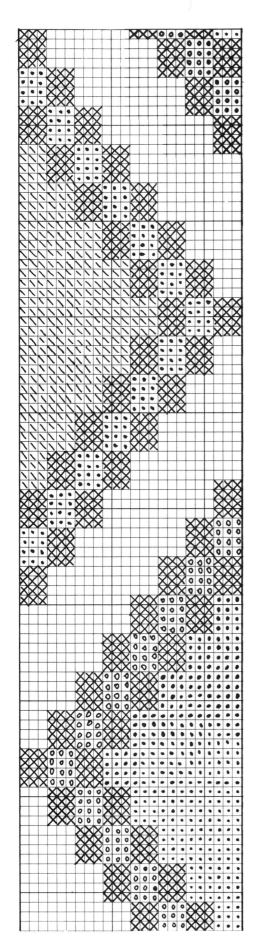

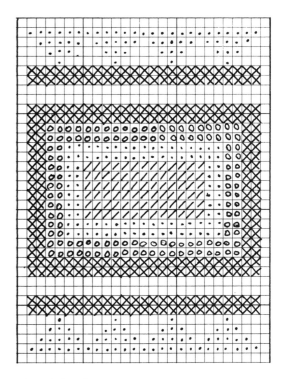

ARAPAHO

Shown in color on the inside front cover.

28 warp threads

COLOR KEY   ⊠ navy blue   ⧄ yellow
          ⊡ red   ⊙ light blue

BLACKFOOT

Shown in color on the inside front cover.

25 warp threads

COLOR KEY   ⊠ navy blue
                 ⊙ yellow
                 ⊡ pink
                 ◩ white
                 background—
                 light blue

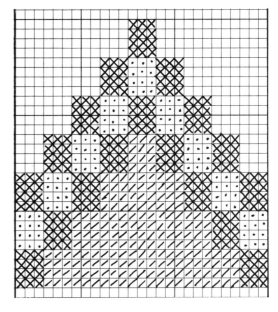

BLACKFOOT

28 warp threads

COLOR KEY   ⧄ yellow   ⊠ black
          ⊡ pink
          background—medium blue

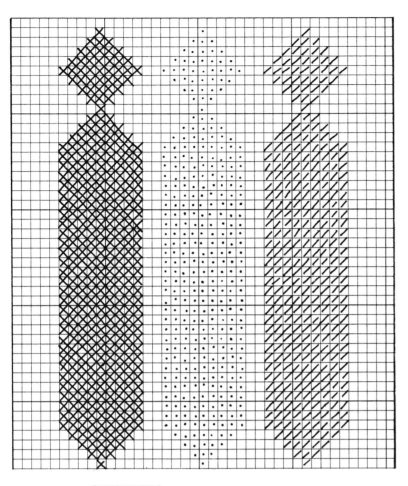

CHIPPEWA

42 warp threads

COLOR KEY   ☒ navy blue   ⊡ orange
              ☑ green

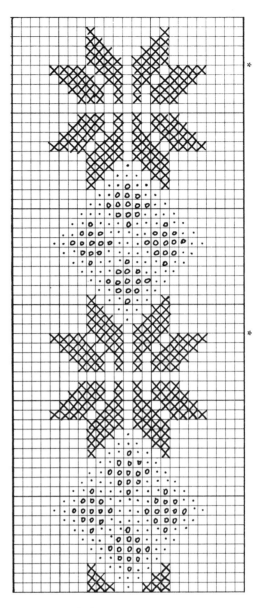

IROQUOIS

26 warp threads

COLOR KEY   ☒ green   ⊡ white
              ◙ purple
              background—light blue

Repeat from * to * for pattern.

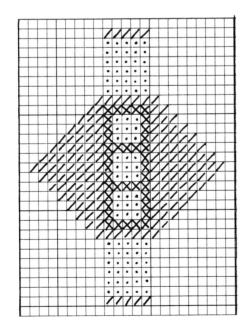

SIOUX

24 warp threads

COLOR KEY   ☑ navy blue   ⊡ red
              ☒ light blue

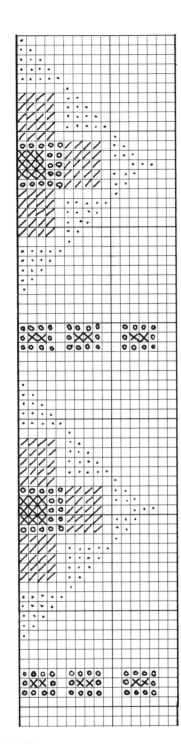

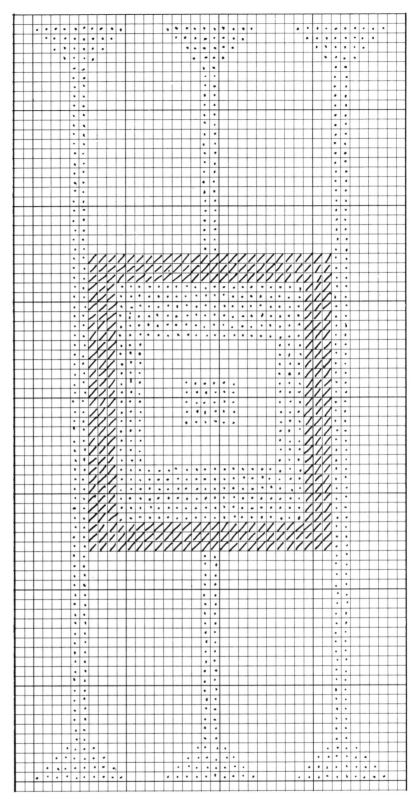

SIOUX

18 warp threads

COLOR KEY   ☒ gold   ⊡ navy blue

⊙ red   ╱ green

DAKOTA SIOUX

43 warp threads

COLOR KEY   ⊡ white   ╱ red

background—navy blue

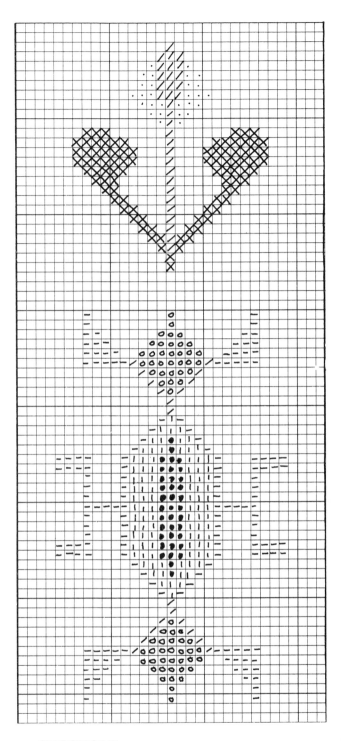

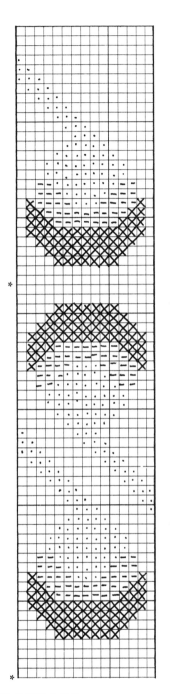

SHOSHONI

34 warp threads

COLOR KEY   ⊠ navy blue   ⊙ medium blue
           ⧄ red   ● brown
           · green   Ⅱ yellow
           ⊟ black

WINNEBAGO

Shown in color on the back cover.

16 warp threads

COLOR KEY   ⊠ navy blue
           · red
           ⊟ yellow

Repeat from * to * for pattern.

WINNEBAGO

10 warp threads

COLOR KEY   ⧄ green

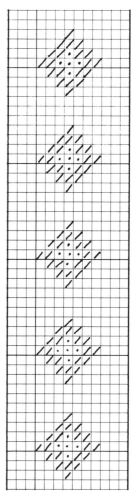

ARIKARA

41 warp threads

COLOR KEY   ☒ red   ⊡ black
  ⊙ blue
  background—yellow

Work from A to B, then from C to
D for one motif.

CHIPPEWA

14 warp threads

COLOR KEY   ⧄ gold
  ⊡ green

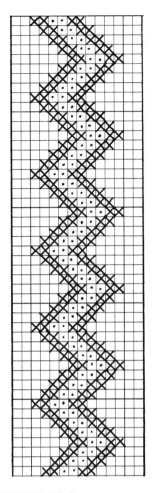

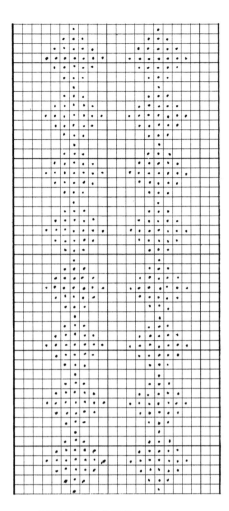

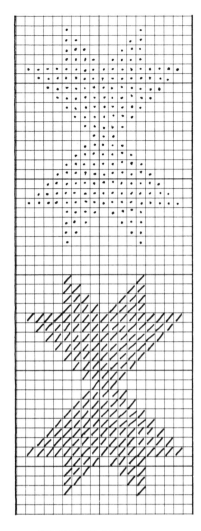

WINNEBAGO

Shown in color on the back cover.

15 warp threads
COLOR KEY ☒ dark green
⬚ ⊡ yellow

WINNEBAGO

23 warp threads
COLOR KEY ⊡ dark green

WINNEBAGO

20 warp threads
COLOR KEY ☑ green
⬚ ⊡ orange

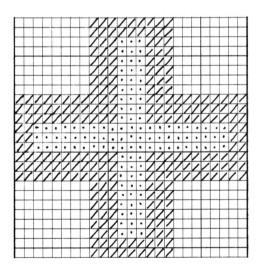

CROW

26 warp threads
COLOR KEY ☑ red   ⊡ yellow
background—light blue

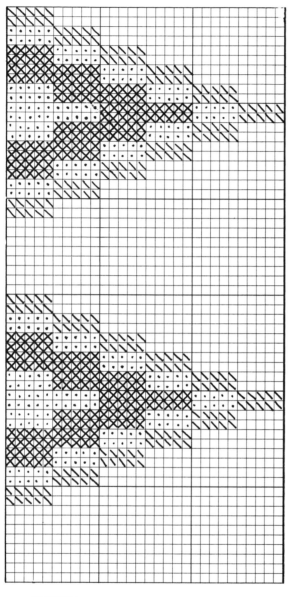

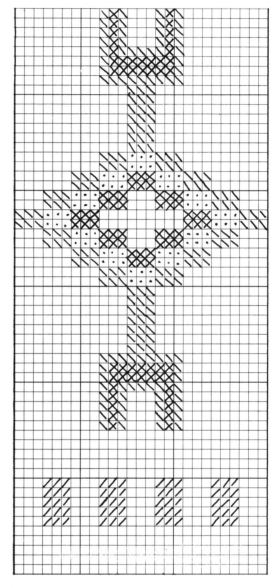

SIOUX

Shown in color on the inside front cover.

31 warp threads

COLOR KEY ◺ navy blue   ⊠ red
         ⊡ light blue

SIOUX

28 warp threads

COLOR KEY ⊡ light blue   ◺ navy blue
         ⊘ medium blue   ⊠ red

POTAWATOMI

Shown in color on the inside back cover.

57 warp threads
COLOR KEY   ☒ red   · black
                      ☑ green

WINNEBAGO

10 warp threads
COLOR KEY   ☑ navy blue
                · pink
                ⊙ red

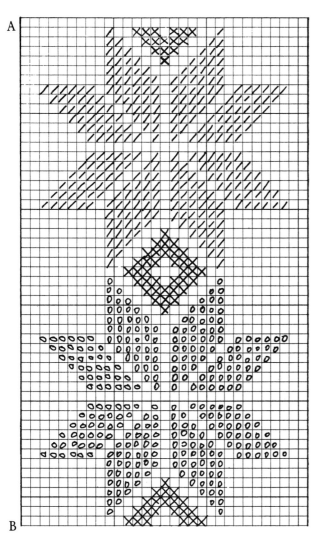

WOODLAND
Shown in color on the back cover.

32 warp threads

COLOR KEY   ☑ black   ☒ green
               ☉ red

Repeat from A to B. Work small center green motif on center repeats only; do not include on first and last star designs.

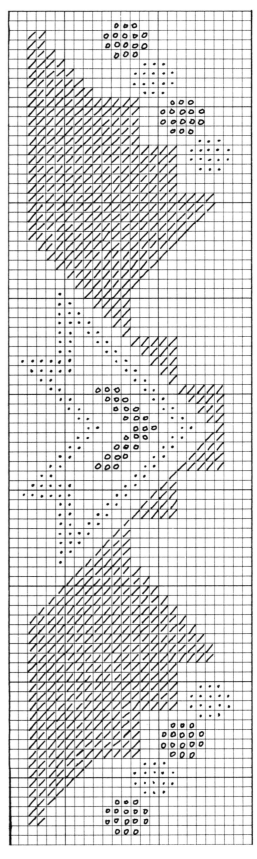

OSAGE

27 warp threads

COLOR KEY   ☑ purple   ⊡ black
               ☉ red

A

Begin *inside* pattern repeat (A to B) here. Continue *border* sequence independently.

B

WOODLAND
Shown in color on the front cover.

84 warp threads

COLOR KEY   ◼ turquoise   ⊡ black
                  ☒ white   ⧄ dark green

Full-Size Patterns for Bead Appliqué

ALGONQUIAN
Shown in color on the inside back cover.

COLOR KEY 1 – wine red   4 – red
2 – dark green   5 – pink
3 – navy blue   6 – medium blue

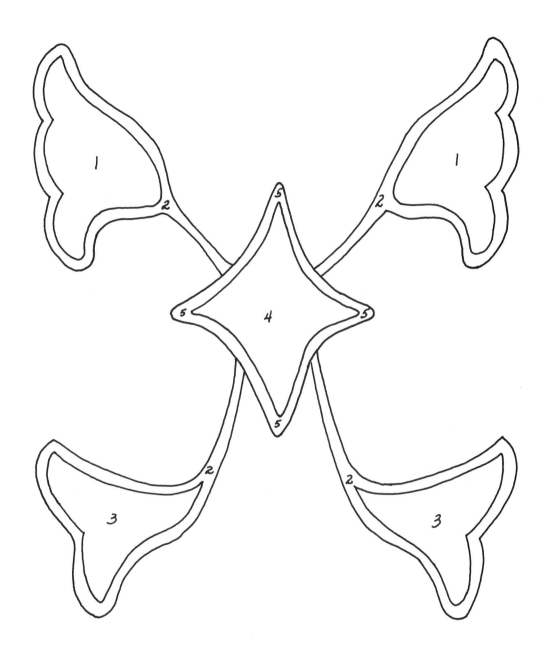

BLACKFOOT

Color Key   1 – pink   4 – light blue
                   2 – navy blue   5 – red
                   3 – yellow

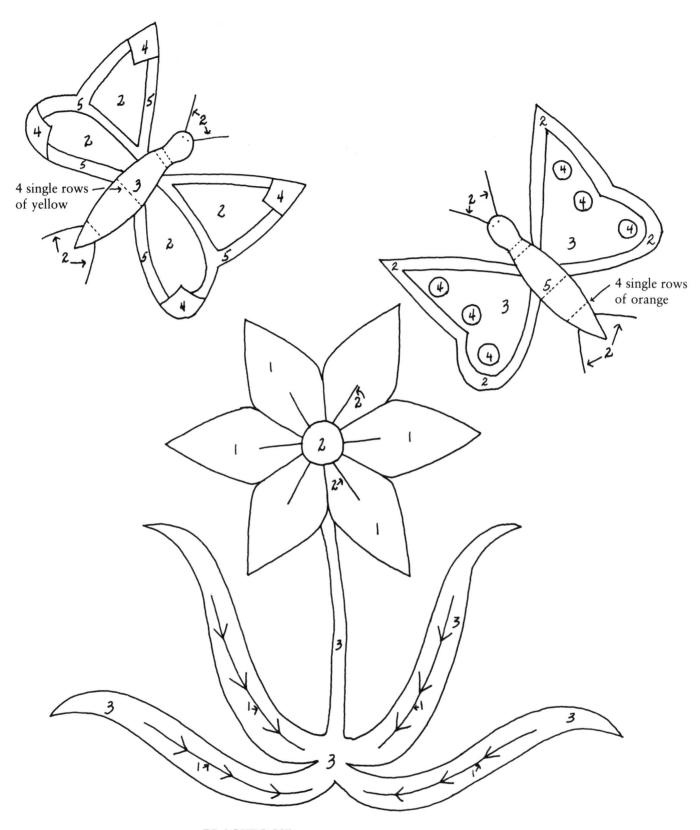

4 single rows of yellow

4 single rows of orange

BLACKFOOT
Shown in color on the front cover.

COLOR KEY   1 – yellow   4 – white
             2 – orange   5 – navy blue
             3 – green
             butterfly eyes—single white beads

CHIPPEWA

Color Key
1 – navy blue   5 – dark green
2 – green   6 – yellow
3 – red   7 – orange
4 – gold

CHIPPEWA

COLOR KEY   1 – gold   4 – navy blue
                2 – dark green   5 – medium blue
                3 – red   6 – white

CHIPPEWA

COLOR KEY 1 – navy blue   6 – white
2 – green   7 – red
3 – light blue   8 – gold
4 – orange   9 – medium blue
5 – dark green

CHIPPEWA

Color Key

1 – medium blue	5 – gray
2 – navy blue	6 – black
3 – red	7 – green
4 – pink	8 – dark green

CHIPPEWA
Lower flower shown on the front cover.

COLOR KEY   1 – white   3 – red
             2 – navy blue   4 – pink

CHIPPEWA

COLOR KEY
1 – dark green
2 – white
3 – pink
4 – red
5 – yellow
6 – gold
7 – light green
8 – light blue
9 – dark blue

CHIPPEWA

Color Key
1 – yellow   6 – red
2 – gold   7 – white
3 – dark green 8 – medium blue
4 – black   9 – transparent red
5 – navy blue

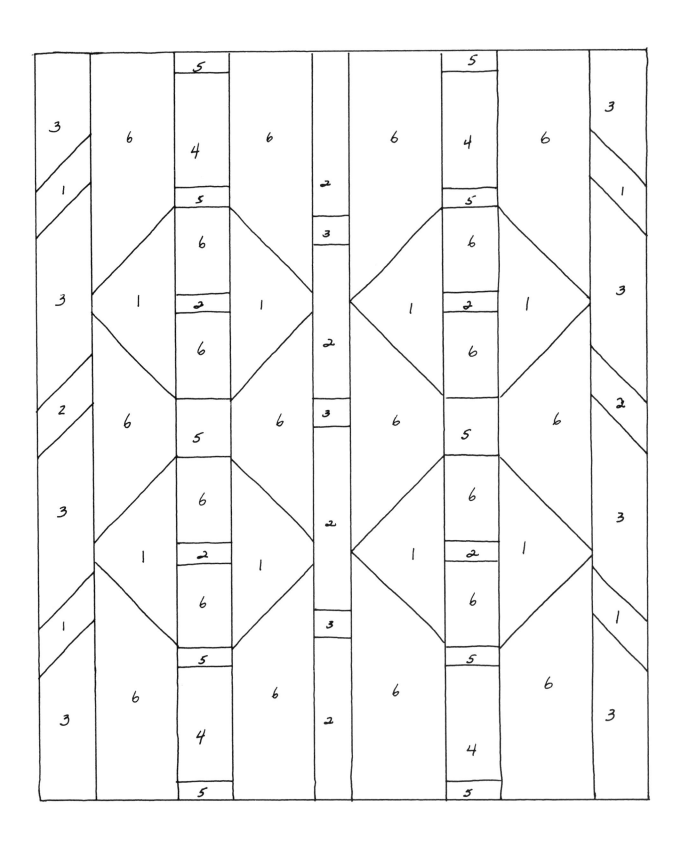

CROW

COLOR KEY   1 – blue   4 – pink
             2 – red   5 – black
             3 – white   6 – light blue

DELAWARE

Shown in color on the front cover.

Color Key   1 – red   3 – medium blue
                    2 – yellow   4 – dark green
                    outline of hearts—single row of white beads

NEZ PERCÉ

Color Key 1 – red   6 – light blue
          2 – green   7 – turquoise
          3 – pink   unnumbered squares—white
          4 – mustard   heavy lines—black
          5 – medium blue

NEZ PERCÉ
Shown in color on the inside back cover.

COLOR KEY   1 – white   4 – dark green
            2 – red   5 – orange
            3 – medium blue   6 – pink

NEZ PERCÉ
Shown in color on the inside back cover.

COLOR KEY
1 – white   4 – light blue
2 – navy blue 5 – rose
3 – black

NEZ PERCÉ
Shown in color on the front cover.

COLOR KEY   1 – navy blue   5 – orange
             2 – red   6 – pink
             3 – green   7 – gold
             4 – yellow

OJIBWA

Color Key
1 – gold
2 – medium blue
3 – light blue
4 – yellow
5 – white
6 – green
7 – dark green

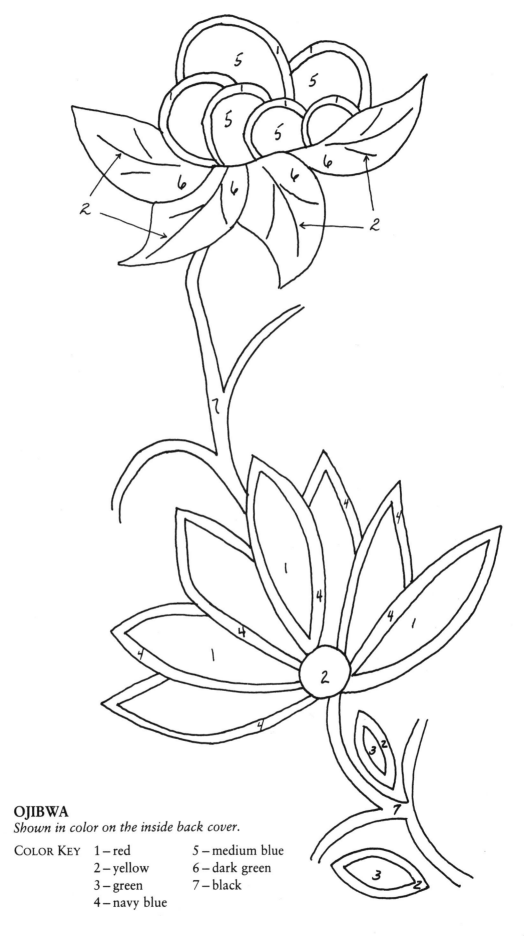

OJIBWA

Shown in color on the inside back cover.

COLOR KEY   1 – red   5 – medium blue
                    2 – yellow   6 – dark green
                    3 – green   7 – black
                    4 – navy blue

OJIBWA
Shown in color on the inside back cover.

COLOR KEY   1 – white   3 – gold   5 – red   7 – dark blue
                 2 – yellow   4 – light blue 6 – pink   8 – mustard

WOODLAND

COLOR KEY
1 – orange	5 – light green
2 – red	6 – navy blue
3 – brown	7 – green
4 – blue	8 – light blue

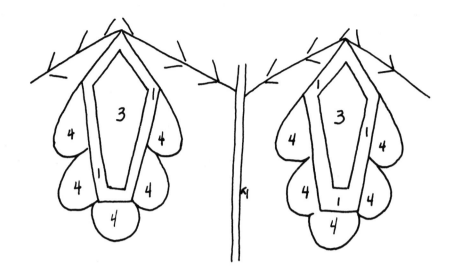

WOODLAND

COLOR KEY   1 – gold   6 – green
                      2 – pink   7 – brown
                      3 – blue   8 – red
                      4 – navy blue   9 – crystal
                      5 – orange   10 – white
                      stems & thorns—white